# SAY THIS--
# NOT THAT!!

For my mother

Thank you for *giving me the words.*

ISBN-13: 978-1463526924

ISBN-10: 146352692X

For more information about the author, visit
http://www.danoconnortraining.com.

Introduction .................................................7

Danger Phrase: "I'm Sorry." ...........................9

Danger Phrase: "Calm down." ......................13

Danger Phrase: "I have an idea." ..................17

Danger Phrase: "What's wrong with you?" ........20

Danger Phrase: "My name is..." ....................24

Danger Phrase: "I disagree." .......................28

Danger Phrase: "Our computers are slow." ........31

Danger Phrase: "Why didn't you tell me?" ........34

Danger Phrase: "But..." ..............................37

Danger Phrase: "Don't take this the wrong way..." ....40

Danger Phrase: "Our policy..." ....................44

Danger Phrase: "I need..." ..........................47

Danger Phrase: "Honestly..." ......................50

Danger Phrase: "You make me..." ................55

Danger Phrase: "No problem!" ....................58

Danger Phrase: "What were you thinking?" ........62

THE Top 4 Power Phrases ............................................66

Danger Phrase: "We need to talk." ..........................71

Power Phrase: "You're in Luck!" ...............................75

Danger Phrase: "You said..." ......................................79

The Most Crucial Phrases of All Time ......................83

# Introduction

Are you ready to become a more powerful, savvy communicator? There's never been an easier, more effective way to do so. Just learn the simple power phrases (to use) and danger phrases (to avoid) that you'll find in this book.

Whether you want to learn one phrase a day or more, the system is as easy as 1-2-3:

**Step 1**: Read the simple danger phrase/power phrase lesson.

**Step 2**: Say the power phrase out loud seven times immediately, and periodically throughout the day. Whisper it quietly to yourself, or use it in conversation, whenever the opportunity arises. Resolve never to use the danger phrases again.

**Step 3**: Keep the quick reference card that accompanies each lesson with you, until you've mastered all the phrases.

Before you begin, take a minute and grab a notebook. In that notebook, make a T-chart and label it DANGER PHRASES and POWER PHRASES like this:

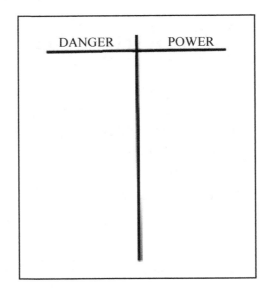

You will be using this *danger phrase* and *power phrase* list with every lesson. This list will become the best communication training tool you've ever had. Once you've done that, you're ready to begin.

For more communication tools and techniques, check out our website, www.danoconnortraining.com, where you'll find free audios, articles, and other tools to help you further improve your communication skills.

Now let's go to your first lesson!

# Lesson 1
# Danger Phrase: "I'm Sorry."

Danger Phrase:

"I'm sorry."

Power Phrase:

"I apologize."

**Theory**:

"I'm sorry," has become basically worthless because the phrase is totally over-used. Furthermore, The more you say "I'm sorry" the more you are likely to diminish your personal power. Think about the people who use this phrase most frequently. They tend to be passive communicators who command little to no respect. Don't make this common communication mistake.

Statistically, women tend to say "I'm sorry" much more than men do, and they shouldn't, because it can be especially disempowering for them. Think about how often you hear women saying they're sorry. For example, women tend to say "I'm sorry" when they don't hear something clearly; they say it when someone steps *on them* at the movie theatre, when someone bumps *their* cart at the grocery store, when they begin a sentence that includes a request ("I'm sorry, could you possibly turn that down?"), when they want to de-fuse a situation, even if the problem is not of their making--and on and on.

These examples make for interesting social experiments. From now on, take note of how often you hear the phrase "I'm sorry," and especially note how often it's said by women. Of course men fall into this trap as well, tending to begin sentences with "I'm sorry, buddy, but...you'll have to'..." Who's buying this? When was the last time one of these "I'm sorry's" made you feel good? Better to say no "sorry" at all. What's almost worse is, when someone deserves a real apology and all they get is an, "I'm really sorry." I mean, really... "I'm sorry?" I think we can do better.

Of course there are occasions when it's appropriate to say, "I'm sorry," such as when you're expressing **sympathy** for someone's loss, or **when you feel bad** about something that happened to someone else ("I'm really sorry you're going through all of this; can I help?") But when you need to apologize for for something you've said or done—the "I apologize" is the only way to go.

## For example, notice the difference:

**SAY THIS**--"I apologize for arriving so late."
**NOT THAT**--"I'm sorry that I arrived so late."

**SAY THIS**--"I apologize for forgetting your birthday."
**NOT THAT**--"I'm sorry I forgot your birthday."

**SAY THIS**--"I apologize for being rude to you in front of your friends."
**NOT THAT**--"I'm sorry I was rude to you in front of your friends."

**Furthermore, a simple, "I was wrong, and I apologize," covers most situations for which you need to apologize. Everyone loves a good old, "You know, Mary, I want you to know I was wrong, and I apologize. It won't happen again." Don't you? There's very little we won't forgive someone for if that's the type of apology they deliver.** Almost everyone finds those words powerful; they will immediately respond positively to them.

Remember, don't offer a tired "I'm sorry" if a *real* apology is truly in order. And if no apology is in order, you shouldn't be saying either "I'm sorry" or "I apologize."

**An important caveat:** Don't ever include the word **"if"** in your apology, as in "I apologize **if....**" If you believe that an apology is warranted, there should be no *if* about it. You've probably had someone say something to you like, "I'm sorry if I offended you," right? If you have, then you know this phrase is just as offensive as whatever happened to warrant that *fake apology*. If you find yourself about to say, "I apologize if..." now you know to stop, and instead say: "I apologize *for*..." and then state what you did.

### For example, notice the difference:

**SAY THIS**--"I apologize **for** hurting your feelings; please forgive me."
**NOT THAT**--"I apologize **if** I hurt your feelings."

**SAY THIS**--"I apologize **for** moving too fast on that."
**NOT THAT**--"I apologize **if** I moved too fast on that."

**SAY THIS**--"I apologize **for** revealing too much information about you."
**NOT THAT**--"I apologize **if** I revealed too much information about you."

## Quick reference card
## #1

# Lesson 2
# Danger Phrase: "Calm down."

Danger Phrase:
"Calm down."

Power Phrase:
"I understand..."

### Theory:

When human beings are emotionally out of control, what we are looking for is validation. We need someone to recognize and validate our emotional state. Frequently, however, when we *encounter* someone who has lost control emotionally, instead of starting off by validating their feelings, we begin by discounting or dismissing those feelings, which only adds fuel to their heightened emotional state. Please notice that validating a person's emotional state is different from agreeing with *the facts* that person is presenting. He or she might be dead wrong in recounting what occurred, but that is not the issue at the moment.

The issue is how to get that person back in mental balance, and capable of reasoning once again. In other words, you want this individual to calm down, but you'll never accomplish this by saying "calm down," which appeals to reason—when the person is operating totally on an emotional level. You may as well be going up to a barking dog and reasoning: "Now calm down, Butch; you are acting way out of control, and you'll never get what you want by barking at me."

Bottom line is this: When someone is communicating from emotion (the right side of the brain), we should start by addressing and validating that emotion *before* addressing any logic (the left side of the brain). The reason is that until you validate and speak to the right side of the brain--which is speaking to you--the left side of the brain won't be able to hear you.

### For example, notice the difference:

**SAY THIS**--"I understand how upset you are, and I can help."
**NOT THAT**--"I can't help you until you calm down!"

**SAY THIS**--"I understand why you would feel that way; please give me a chance to help."
**NOT THAT**--"Please calm down and I'll be able to help you."

**Furthermore, don't make the mistake of using the danger phrase, "I understand *how* you feel."** When we say that, people tend to think (*or often say*), "*No you don't! How could you possibly know how I feel?*" and we have made matters even worse.

What we mean to say is, "I understand **why** you'd feel that way." Saying this simply conveys the idea that we understand the chain of events that have led to the person feeling the way they feel. We can't understand *how* they feel, because we are not that person, but we can understand *why* they feel the way they do.

**For example, notice the difference:**

**SAY THIS**--"I can certainly understand why you'd be so upset."
**NOT THAT**--"I understand exactly how you feel."

A quick note—you are neither agreeing nor disagreeing with the facts as the other person sees them. You are dealing strictly with understanding the feelings—the emotions—the upset—of the other person. Once you've validated the *person*, you'll find it easier to deal with the *facts* and resolve the problem. When people "feel" better—when they feel validated—sometimes that validation itself solves the problem. Many times people simply want to be *heard*. Think about your latest experience with customer service representatives, and compare those who genuinely listened and cared, with those who did neither.... How important is it to you to be understood?

## Quick reference card
## #2

# Lesson 3
# Danger Phrase: "I have an idea."

Danger Phrase:

"I have an idea."


Power Phrase:

"I have an answer."

## Theory:

If you have a great idea--perhaps about how things could
be done better, or how a problem can be solved, or how a
product could improve one's life or living conditions, don't
make the mistake most people do—of presenting it simply
as *a good idea*. When people have problems, they don't want
*ideas*; they want **answers**. When you have an *answer* to a
problem or a challenge, be sure to call it what it really is,
and don't diminish your answers by calling them ideas.
Nobody wants to hear random ideas; everyone wants to
hear specific answers.

Additionally, people associate us with others who speak the
way we speak. The moment we open our mouths and start
talking, people connect us and associate us with others who
speak the way we do. You want to be associated with
powerful, savvy communicators who are strong, dynamic,

problem-solvers with **answers**. We all know people who have a lot of ideas...a lot of useless ideas that won't or shouldn't become reality. People who present useless ideas in a weak manner are too often perceived to be weak and ineffective. Don't put yourself in this category. Choose words wisely, making certain they are both precise and powerful.

### For example, notice the difference:

**SAY THIS**--"I have the answer to this problem."
**NOT THAT**--"I have an idea about how we can fix this problem."

**SAY THIS**--"I have an answer I believe will work."
**NOT THAT**--"I have an idea I think will work."

**Furthermore, as you might have noticed above, the word *believe* is preferable to the word *think*.** This adds extra power and credibility to your message. *Thinking* something is different from *believing* something. You want to state unequivocally that you believe in your own solutions.

Of course, you can also substitute the words *solution* or *proposal* for *answer* if you believe them to be more appropriate for the occasion. Both of these are words that powerful, savvy communicators would use instead of the word *idea*.

## For example, notice the difference:

**SAY THIS**--"I've come up with a few proposals for you."
**NOT THAT**--"I've come up with a few ideas for you."

**SAY THIS**--"I believe I have the solution."
**NOT THAT**--"I think I have an idea."

Think about it: Would you prefer to do business with the person offering you solutions or the person offering you ideas?

## Quick reference card
## #3

# Lesson 4
# Danger Phrase: "What's wrong with you?"

Danger Phrase:
"What's wrong with you?"


Power Phrase:
"What's bothering you?"


**Theory:**

We generally say the danger phrase "What's wrong with you?" to people when they are visibly upset and we want them to tell us what the problem is. The challenge is that people don't like to admit that there is something wrong *with them*. People don't, however, mind acknowledging that there is something **bothering** them; this is quite different from acknowledging that something is wrong *with them*. The danger phrase implies the person is a part of the problem, and the speaker's inflection frequently accentuates this, as in "What's wrong with **you**?" And it's no better when the speaker says: "What's **wrong** with you?" because listeners may well become defensive at the thought that there's something wrong with their thinking, or they are not being rational—in other words, they may feel they are being told they don't **have** a problem, but that they **are** the problem.

Additionally, if you don't know the person well, a simple, "Is there something bothering you?" might be enough. Some people like to talk about their troubles; some don't. Most people, however, modify their behavior and tend to act more normally when they know that someone has noticed that they are out-of-sorts. Asking if there's something bothering a person does just that; it lets the person know that their troubles are noticed even if they don't want to talk about them.

### For example, notice the difference:

**SAY THIS**--"What's bothering you so much that you would say that?"
**NOT THAT**--"Why would you say that? What's wrong with you?"

**SAY THIS**--"What's upsetting you?"
**NOT THAT**--"What's your problem?"

**Furthermore, as you might have noticed above, the phrase, "What's your problem?" is just as bad as, "What's wrong with you?"** Both of them tend to get the same reaction--a defensive one. If what you're looking for is to actually get to the *root* of someone's problem, changing just a few words will help you do so much more effectively.

One last note: When someone initially denies that anything is wrong when it's obvious that there is something wrong, instead of saying, "Do you want to talk about it? Are you sure?" Simply say, "I'm here for you if you want to talk about it." This lets the person know that you are available when they are ready to talk. Some people need time to figure out *how they feel*, and if they have already said they don't want to talk, they might feel as though the door has been closed. Telling someone, "I'm here for you if you want to talk about it," leaves the door open without putting pressure on anyone.

**For example, notice the difference:**

**SAY THIS**--"I'm here for you, if you ever want to talk about it."
**NOT THAT**--"Do you want to talk about it?" (*Assume a "No."*) "Are you sure??"

Which person would you go to when you really do want to talk about it? Especially when it comes to your family, never simpy ask "Do you want to talk about it?" and then go away if the answer is "No." Always keep that communication door wide open, especially in your primary relationships.

## Quick reference card
## #4

# Lesson 5
# Danger Phrase: "My name is..."

Danger Phrase:

"My name is..."

Power Phrase:

"I'm..."

**Theory:**

Our introduction of ourselves says a lot about who we think we are. If you listen to people introduce themselves, you'll notice that those who consider themselves successful and important start out with "I'm" rather than "My name is." If you want to project more confidence and power, speak like those who project confidence and power--and start your introduction with "I'm...."

Additionally, if you *do* want to come off as more passive rather than assertive (for example if you encounter a scared child in the mall), it would be appropriate to say, "My name is..." in order to make the other person feel more at ease.

**For example, notice the difference:**

**SAY THIS**--"Hi, I'm Dan O'Connor."
**NOT THAT**--"Hi, my name's Dan O'Connor."

**SAY THIS**--"It's nice to meet you Mary; I'm Dan."
**NOT THAT**--"It's nice to meet you Mary; my name's Dan."

**Furthermore, on the telephone**, you want to say, "This is Dan," rather than, "My name's Dan."

**SAY THIS**--"Hi, this is Dan O'Connor, with Power Diversity; is Mary in?"
**NOT THIS**--"Hi, My name's Dan O'Connor, with Power Diversity; is Mary in?"

**SAY THIS**--"Hi Mark, this is Jim Schmith, Commercial Realtor with Goldmark."
**NOT THIS**-- "Hi Mark, my name is Jim Schmith. I'm a Commercial Realtor with Goldmark."

These are subtle but important distinctions, if you wish to separate yourself from the pack, especially in business. Picture, if you will, some person of prestige or power—for example, the governor of your state, calling to ask for your vote. If Governor George Mayview called you, would he say: "Hi, my name is George Mayview, and I'd appreciate your vote in the fall"?  Or would he say: "Hi, this is George Mayview, and I'd appreciate your vote in the fall"? George's assumption is that you already know who he is because he's a high-profile person of position and power, so he'd begin with **"Hi, this is…"** (in other words—*you know me—the governor—doesn't everybody know me??*) If Oprah Winfrey called your home, would she begin with: "Hello, my name is Oprah Winfrey, and…" No way. She would begin with: "Hello, this is Oprah Winfrey calling," making the assumption that you know her because—*doesn't everybody??* She would project the confidence of a person of power and recognition.

Take note and do the same, if you want to be seen as confident and successful. "My name is…" is a passive introduction of an unknown person who is acknowledging he/she is not important enough to be well-known. As Joseph Kennedy told his sons: "Image is as important as reality, boys; project the right image." Whether this is a good thing is debatable, but whether it is *true* is not debatable.

One other thing—when you are on the phone, make certain that your voice is strong and firm.  Practice speaking from the diaphragm. A strong voice coupled with: **"Hi John, this is Jim Schmith, Commercial Realtor with**

**Goldmark"** results in the listener thinking he probably knows you, or if not, he should.

Before you make your next call, or personal introduction, practice this script, and make certain that your tone is confident without being over-bearing. You'll command the respect you deserve and be remembered by those whose paths you cross.

## Quick reference card
## #5

# Lesson 6
# Danger Phrase: "I disagree."

Danger Phrase:

"I disagree."

Power Phrase:

"I see it another way."

**Theory:**

We all disagree with other people. The savvy communicator, however, knows how to disagree with someone without *fighting*. Most people begin with: "Well I disagree," and we know what that creates--a situation in which the person hearing "I disagree" wants to prove the speaker wrong. If you're not interested in a good argument, and simply want to go on record as having a difference of opinion, choose your opening words carefully, because, as you know--words make all the difference. And opening words set the tone for whatever follows.

Additionally, what we say to other people creates a bio-chemical reaction in the people to whom we're speaking. When we say to someone, "I disagree," chemicals are released in the brain to help people "fight it out," and argue the point; they become more aggressive. Instead of talking

28

about whether you agree or not, if you simply state the way you look at things, this will not cause the same aggression-producing chemical reaction.

### For example, notice the difference:

**SAY THIS**--"I understand what you're saying; I simply see it another way."
**NOT THAT**--"I understand what you're saying; I just disagree."

**SAY THIS**--"I understand how you see it; I simply see it differently."
**NOT THAT**--"You make a good point, but I disagree with you."

**SAY THIS**--"I see it differently, however this is interesting; tell me more if you like."
**NOT THAT**--"I totally disagree."

**Furthermore, if your goal is to voice disagreement, while *surrendering* to the other person, do it the right way**; use the phrase, "I trust your judgment, and you have my support." You should use this phrase as often as possible, because the more you say it, the more people trust *your* judgment and support *you*. If you are someone who doesn't normally *surrender*, try doing so more often, and watch how support for you and your ideas will grow.

**Please note**: One of the most passive-aggressive danger phrases—one that invariably provokes a negative, confrontational response—one that is truly a wolf in sheep's clothing is—**"Let's just agree to disagree."** We all know that these are fighting words. Unless you're looking to aggravate the listener, this is a **delete** phrase.

### For example, notice the difference:

**SAY THIS--**"I can understand how you see it; I see it another way; however I trust your judgement and you have my support."
**NOT THIS--**"Let's just agree to disagree."

When you use power phrases such as the ones suggested, not only do you minimize the listener's counter-productive aggression, but he or she will see things your way more often because you will be seen as more fair and flexible. People in general are more fair and flexible with those whom they see as fair and flexible.

## Quick reference card
## #6

# Lesson 7

# Danger Phrase: "Our computers are slow."

Danger Phrase:

"Our Computers are slow."


Power Phrase:

"While we're waiting for the computer to process...."


### Theory:

Normally we say this to our customers while we're serving them over the telephone. Why would we want to tell our customers that we have inferior computer systems any more than we would tell them that we are incompetent? We have all had customer service agents tell us that their computers are slow. Has it ever inspired more confidence in--or loyalty to--the agent or the company? Of course not.

Additionally, when we are serving our customers, the number one thing we should be focused on is not our technical job, but instead we should be focusing on establishing the P-E-C (personal-emotional-connection). Any opportunity we have to make the P-E-C is valuable, and if our computers are slow or down, this is a perfect moment to establish or *further* establish it.

**For example, notice the difference:**

**SAY THIS**--"While we're waiting for the computer to process, tell me, how has your experience with us been so far?"
**NOT THAT**--"I'm sorry; our computers are really slow today."

**SAY THIS**--"While this is pulling up, tell me more about the house you're buying."
**NOT THAT**--"Just a minute; our computers are slow today."

**SAY THIS**--"While the information is coming up, could you please tell me why you chose to work with us?"
**NOT THAT**--"Please give me a minute while the computer comes up."

**Furthermore, the more often you establish the P-E-C,** the more patient customers will be with you, and the more they'll forgive technical difficulties. Everyone works with computers, and everyone understands slow computers. Most customer service people think there is nothing they can do about it, but there is--they can use it as an opportunity.

### For example, notice the difference:

**SAY THIS**--"Unfortunately our computers are down, but fortunately you got me, Dan O'Connor, and I'm going to help you as best I can. Tell me about...."
**NOT THAT**--"Unfortunately our computers are down right now."

When you use opportunities such as computers being down or slow to establish the P-E-C, what you're really doing is establishing *yourself* as a powerful, savvy communicator.

## Quick reference card #7

# Lesson 8
# Danger Phrase: "Why didn't you tell me?"

Danger Phrase:
"Why didn't you tell me?"


Power Phrase:
"In the future, you can always come to me with these things."


**Theory:**

We've all had people reveal things to us that make us think or say, "Why didn't you tell me?" or "Why didn't you tell me earlier?"

However, when someone says "Why didn't you tell me?" to us, our answer is almost always the same--We were embarrassed or we were afraid of the repercussions of our revelation, or we didn't want to cause a bigger problem than we already had. In the future, when you are about to ask someone why they didn't tell you something, just assume that the reason has to do with fear, embarrassment, or not wanting to hurt you. (Of course sometimes people refrain from telling something because they are skeptical about what that other person will do with the information.) Instead of compounding the feelings of the other person with shame, the message we really mean to convey to that person is one of security and comfort. What we want to say is—*"Hey, I am here for you, without judgment, to help you with whatever is troubling you. You can tell me anything and trust me with the information."* When the other person receives that message, he or she will undoubtedly be more forthcoming and open in the future.

Additionally, since our message is *"You can come to me anytime, with anything"* it's best to be clear and direct—and simply say that.

### For example, notice the difference:

**SAY THIS**--"You know, in the future, you can always come to me with these things."
**NOT THAT**--"Why didn't you tell me what was going on?"

**SAY THIS**--"In the future, I hope you know you can always tell me how you feel."
**NOT THAT**--"Why didn't you tell me how you felt?"

**Furthermore, it's always good to let others know that we won't judge them.** We confide more in people who are non-judgmental. We trust more in people who are non-judgmental. If you want people to trust and confide *in you more*, tell people you are worthy of trust and confidence. One way of doing so is to let people know you won't judge them. And then—*don't judge them*.... That is the hard part.

**For example, notice the difference:**

**SAY THIS--**"In the future, you can always come to me with these things and know that I won't
judge you when you do."
**NOT THAT--**"Why didn't you tell me what you were doing?"

When your objective is clear—e.g. conveying the message to others that communicating with you is safe--power phrases such as the ones listed above will help you achieve your objective more quickly and easily.

## Quick reference card
## #8

# Lesson 9
# Danger Phrase: "But..."

Danger Phrase:

"But..."

Power Phrase:

"Having said that..."

## Theory:

We've all heard sentences that start out with nice things that we want to hear, such as, "Dan, I've always enjoyed working with you, and think you're an excellent teacher." And we've all experienced those nice thoughts followed by the dreaded, "BUT...." And of course that big "But" negated the entire preceding message—at least in our minds. Take for example: "I really enjoyed your presentation, **but** it went on too long." Hard to imagine that the person speaking *really* enjoyed the presentation, right? Be careful not to put a *but* after a compliment, if your intention is to truly compliment the person.

Additionally, there are certain phrases used exclusively by savvy communicators--phrases that novice communicators simply don't use. "Having said that..." is one of these phrases. Simply saying, "Having said that..." *connects* you with other people who say this phrase. If you look and listen, you'll note that this phrase is used frequently by news anchors, talk show hosts, and other trained, professional, savvy communicators. The more you talk like a savvy communicator, the more people will see you in that light. "Having said that" tells the listener you meant what you said—you are not retracting it—however there is more to be communicated. It is far smoother than the very abrupt "but...."

## For example, notice the difference:

**SAY THIS**--"I trust you. Having said that, I can't do what you're asking."
**NOT THAT**--"I trust you, **but** I can't do what you're asking."

**SAY THIS**--"I've always enjoyed working with you. That said, I have to move on."
**NOT THAT**--"I've always enjoyed working with you, **but** I have to move on."

**SAY THIS**--"I understand what you're saying. Having said that, I see it another way."
**NOT THAT**--"I understand what you're saying, **but** I simply disagree." (Notice the violation of this lesson and lesson 6.)

**Furthermore, a great way to avoid this situation is to simply place a "while" at the beginning of the sentence.**

**For example, notice the difference:**

**SAY THIS--**"While I understand why you'd say that, I simply see it differently."

**NOT THAT--**"I understand why you'd say that, **but** I disagree. (Notice the violation of this lesson and lesson 6.)

**SAY THIS--**"While I understand why you'd say that, I simply see it differently.

**NOT THAT--**"I understand why you'd say that, **but** I don't agree with you.

**SAY THIS--**"While I love you, I can't do that for you."
**NOT THAT--**"I love you, **but** I can't do that for you."

One last note on the *but*. "I love you, **but**..." is **never** OK. This is what we call a delete phrase or purge phrase. A *but* **never comes after "I love you." Never.**

## Quick reference card
## #9

# Lesson 10
# Danger Phrase: "Don't take this the wrong way..."

Danger Phrase:

"No offense but..."

"Don't take this the wrong way but..."

"I don't mean to be rude but..."

Power Phrase:

There is no power phrase you can use to replace these; they are simply **DELETE** phrases.

### Theory:

We've all heard people start sentences with, "No offense but..." and the moment we hear this, we can feel a visceral reaction creeping up; we get defensive, nervous, angry, aggressive, or perhaps just queasy. In any event, nothing good has ever come after, "No offense but." Nothing good —ever—and the listener always knows it, as does the speaker.

Additionally, if we know we are about to say something that is offensive, hurtful, or rude, the correct thing to do is simply recognize that fact, and say *nothing at all.* Prefacing the offensive comment with "no offense but" does not then absolve the speaker for the responsibility of the pain he or she is about to inflict.

Remember--as assertive communicators it is NOT our obligation to say everything that comes into our heads, or everything that we think needs to be said. Instead, as assertive, *savvy* communicators, we do our cost-benefit analysis before speaking. No real benefit accrues to us or anyone else from saying offensive, insulting, or hurtful things. Our ego might feel temporarily gratified, but in the end, this kind of communication doesn't serve anyone.

### For example, notice the difference:

"No offense, but you look awful in that outfit," vs. *nothing at all.*

"Don't take this the wrong way, but I don't think he likes you very much," vs. *nothing at all.*

"I don't mean to be rude, but nobody here cares," vs. *nothing at all.*

**Furthermore, there are ways to deliver constructive criticism when necessary**. One of the easiest ways to deliver effective constructive criticism is to do so using the "Criticize with Compliments" technique. You can almost always use the same lead-in line, which is "You're too...to let..."

**For example, notice the difference:**

**SAY THIS--**"You're too polished a professional to let something like a personality conflict
tarnish your image."
**NOT THAT--**"You need to stop fighting with Trixie."

**SAY THIS--**"You've worked too hard on this report to let errors distract from the message."
**NOT THIS--** "This report is full of errors."

You'll notice you NEVER begin with "Don't take this personally" nor should you begin with a compliment followed by "but," as was discussed in the previous lesson. Do not give a compliment and then criticize—(which is what happens when you say something glowing, followed by "but.") Instead make the compliment *itself* the message. It is possible to criticize with compliments, if you practice this technique and make it your own. You will be amazed at how effective this positive, encouraging approach can be.

A savvy communicator knows how to deliver constructive criticism, and also knows when it's best to say *nothing at all.*

## Quick reference card
## #10

# Lesson 11
# Danger Phrase: "Our policy..."

Danger Phrase:

"Our policy..."

Power Phrase:

"The reason our policy states _____ is

because..."

### Theory:

We've all been aggravated by customer service agents telling us what their company policy is. While we can understand that mere mortals don't have the power to override company policy, *the way* someone tells us about company rules can make all the difference in how we feel about hearing the bad news. Furthermore, we can all more easily accept rules and regulations when we understand the reason they were implemented in the first place.

Basically, simply telling someone that "it's our company policy" is the equivalent of saying, "Because I said so."

And nobody ever likes to hear that, do they?

If you are a customer service representative, you are aware of the policies, rules, and regulations of your company. You are aware of *when* you have to tell customers about these rules. But are you aware of the *reasons* for each policy? What is the logic behind each and every one? Learn the reasons so that you can explain them to the customer, avoiding the word *policy* whenever possible. If you must use the dreaded word *policy*, explain the *reason* for having such a policy, while you're telling customers about it.

## For example, notice the difference:

**SAY THIS**--"I understand this can be frustrating, but we have these procedures in place to protect your account from fraud. That's why we ask you to deliver your application in person for your protection."

**NOT THAT**--"I'm sorry, but our company policy states you must deliver your application in person rather than by fax or mail—no exceptions."

**SAY THIS**--"Unfortunately, we have to have uniform policies like this so we can keep your rates as low as possible."

**NOT THAT**--"Company policy states that if you don't pay your bill by the 7th, your service will be cut off."

**Furthermore, you might have noticed that in the examples given above, the policy was explained so that it is a benefit to the customer.** It is your job as a savvy communicator to find a way to always stress the benefit to the customer.

### For example, notice the difference:

**SAY THIS--**"To ensure your own safety, I have to insist you wear this orange hard hat. We wouldn't want anything to happen to you while you're with us."
**NOT THAT--**"You have to wear this hat to enter the construction site. It's company policy."

One last note: Remember that when you have to deliver news that will be frustrating for the recipient to hear, you should always try and find the person's WIIFM (What's in it for me?). Doing so will make you seem less like the bearer of bad news, and more like a human being who cares—or at the very least you will be both.

## Quick reference card
## #11

# Lesson 12
# Danger Phrase: "I need..."

Danger Phrase:

"I need..."

Power Phrase:

*Place the real subject at the beginning of the sentence.*

### Theory:

**"I need that report by the end of the day."** What part of that sentence was given the most importance and emphasis? If you said "I need," you'd be correct. What was *really* the most important thing in that sentence that *should have been* emphasized? *The report,* right?

Many novice communicators make the mistake of misplacing the **real** subject of their sentences. Always remember that the power in your sentence lives *at the beginning* of your sentence. Whatever you place as the subject (normally at the beginning) has the most power, and is what you are really emphasizing, wittingly or unwittingly. You'll notice the verbal patterns of powerful, savvy, professional communicators very rarely begin with "I need" unless their needs really are the most important part of the message they're sending.

## For example, notice the difference:

**SAY THIS--**"That report is due by the end of the day."
**NOT THAT--**"I need that report by the end of the day."

**SAY THIS--**"This class deserves your full attention."
**NOT THAT--**"You need to pay attention in class."

**Furthermore, as we have learned in previous chapters, if you want to be seen as a savvy, polished, powerful professional, you must speak like one.** This means you must begin to seriously think about your message before you attempt to deliver it. It also means practicing, with deliberation, the scripts, phrases, and lead-in lines you intend to use in your conversations. In this case, think carefully about what you would like to stress, and begin your sentences with those words and ideas. Practice eliminating or reducing the "I need" from the beginning of your sentences. You'll find that the listener will key in on what you are asking him/her to do, because you are keying in on it.

## For example, notice the difference:

**SAY THIS--**"Your complete focus is vital to the success of this project."

**NOT THAT--**"I need you to really focus on this project."

Again, if the emphasis is truly on your needs, and this is sometimes the case—such as *"I need a ride to the doctor tomorrow at noon; can you help me out?"* then—and only then—is it OK to lead with your need.

One last note especially for women: Women more than men need to be careful not to start sentences in the workplace that begin with "I need." The reason? Women, much more than men, when using this phrase, tend to find themselves labeled as *"needy."*

## Quick reference card
## #12

# Lesson 13
# Danger Phrase: "Honestly..."

Danger Phrase:
"Honestly..." or "To be honest..."

Power Phrase:
"Frankly..."

**Theory:**

Why do we feel the need to tell people we're being honest?
Doesn't this imply that otherwise, we're being dishonest?
Why would we have to alert people to our honesty? Even
worse is asking "Do you want me to be completely honest
with you?" Is the implication that if the listener says "Yes,"
we will continue on—telling the truth. But if the listener
says "No," we'll continue on—lying. What's up with that
question??

The bottom line is, we shouldn't have to tell people when
we're being honest; that ought to be the assumption. People
should certainly be able to rely on the fact that if we're
communicating, we're doing it honestly. The more we say
things such as, "honestly..." the more we appear to be less
than genuine. Furthermore, most of the time when we say
things such as, "Well, if you want my honest opinion..."

what we really mean to say is something more along the lines of, "If you want me to be frank with you..." We say "frank" in preparation for the expression of feelings or opinions that might not be well-received. It's a polite way of saying: "You asked—and I'm going to tell you; please don't shoot the messenger."

There's a difference between honesty and frankness. Honesty is truth-telling, and frankness is openness. You can be honest, without being frank—meaning what you say is the truth, as far as you take it, but you aren't volunteering much. You might be holding back a little or a lot. You aren't necessarily being very open. But if you are being frank, you are ipso facto being fully honest as well. You can't be frank and lie at the same time. Additionally, the word "frank" is rarely used by novice communicators, and is frequently used by powerful, savvy communicators. Again, if you want to be seen as a savvy, powerful communicator, start talking like one.

**Furthermore, when powerful people *do* begin a sentence with "honestly," they diminish their personal power in the eyes of the listener.** Consider your own reaction to politicians or salespeople who begin sentences with "honestly" or "to be honest." If you hear this too much, you might wonder—"Who is he/she trying to convince??" If you hear the word "honestly" too often from the mouth of the same person, it has the exact opposite effect of the one the speaker intends. That is precisely why savvy communicators try to avoid the word in any form.

**For example, notice the difference:**

**SAY THIS**--"Frankly, it's difficult for me to see how this is going to work."
**NOT THAT**--"Honestly, it's difficult for me to see how this is going to work."

**SAY THIS**--"Would you like me to be frank?" (The answer might be "No, I'm not really ready to fully discuss this with you," but if the answer is "Yes" you've been given permission to fully voice your views.)
**NOT THAT**--"Would you like me to be honest?" (The question is hollow because a "No" is inconceivable.)

ALERT! ALERT! "I'm just being honest" is a danger phrase that invariably is an attempt to cover rudeness. It is a passive-aggressive sentence that generally comes from the mouth of someone who has chosen, at that moment, to be mean-spirited, and therefore an ineffective communicator. There is normally a way to be honest and direct without being offensive. That's one reason to choose words carefully, isn't it—so we can be effective and forthright without offending people? If you ever find yourself hearing "I'm just being honest" I can guarantee you that someone has just offended you, and is trying to play the innocent. If *you* ever find yourself about to say something like "Well it's the truth! I'm just being honest"—reflect instead about what you said that required that cover-up comment. Were you "just being honest" or were you making an observation or judgment that was not asked for, or was harsh or rude? (OK, let's be frank—if you've put on a few pounds, you don't invite the observation, do you? And if someone comments on **the truth** that you've put on a few, is the blow softened by "I was just being honest!"?

### For example, notice the difference:

**SAY THIS--**"I liked the way the report was laid out. Next time I'd use primary colors rather than fluorescent colors because they're easier on the eyes." (**Please note there is no "but" in this sentence....**)
**NOT THAT--**"I hated the fluorescent colors. I'd get rid of them and use primary colors instead. I'm just being honest."

Bonus: If you are looking to give constructive criticism and are struggling to find the words, use the simple LB/NT (liked best/next time) system, as was used above. Just say what you liked (yes, you have to find something), and say what you would do differently the next time. It's an easy way to ensure that you are truly being *constructive* in your criticism.

## Quick reference card
## #13

# Lesson 14
# Danger Phrase: "You make me..."

Danger Phrase:
"You make me..."

Power Phrase:
"When you...I feel...because..."

### Theory:

First of all, nobody makes us *anything*. We might *feel* a
certain way as a result of someone's behavior, but when we
are angry, hurt, disappointed, or *whatever*, no one is **making**
us feel a certain way. This is simply how we feel. Not only is
saying "you make me..." incorrect, it is extremely
disempowering for the speaker.

**Furthermore, what we are really trying to do is
communicate our feelings**. Unfortunately, this isn't
natural for most human beings. We *struggle* to communicate
our feelings in an assertive, clear, and direct manner,
especially when we are emotionally charged, or when we
believe someone has hurt us. The verbal pattern, "When
you...I feel...because..." might seem simple, but it is very
rarely used. When it is used, you'll note that it's used
exclusively by savvy communicators.

Additionally, you may think that you expressed your feelings **clearly** in the past, but chances are that unless you were specifically using this tactical verbal pattern, you didn't. Remember that we *think* we're saying something--other than what we're really saying--over 50% of the time. This is why--when it really matters--don't wing it! Use your tools, and you'll increase the likelihood that you're actually saying *what you mean to say.*

### For example, notice the difference:

**SAY THIS**--"When you don't do what you say you'll do, I feel disappointed and hurt because I
love you and try to do what I tell you I'll do."
**NOT THAT**--"You know, you really make me mad when you don't do what you say you're going to do."

**SAY THIS**--"When you talk to me like that--calling me names--in front of our friends, I feel embarrassed and humiliated because it reminds me of when I was name called on the playground as a child.."
**NOT THAT**--"That really pisses me off when you do that!"

One last thing: When it comes time to tell people how you feel, try and use words that express not just *how* you feel, but *why* you feel that way. For example, "I feel angry" is common. If you want someone to really *get it*, think of why you're angry and say that. For example, "I feel angry because I feel as though I've been betrayed" is very different from the simple "I feel angry." Also--"I'm hurt," is not nearly as strong as "I feel hurt because I feel as though I'm being abandoned." If you really dig one level deeper, and express why you feel the emotion you feel, people will understand more, and it is when people understand one another that the lines of communication truly open up.

### For example, notice the difference:

**SAY THIS**--"When you talk to me that way, I feel hurt and wounded, because name-calling is abusive. I don't talk that way to you, because I love you, and don't want to hurt you."
**NOT THAT**--"Boy, you can be a jerk."

## Quick reference card
## #14

# Lesson 15
# Danger Phrase: "No problem!"

Danger Phrase:
"No problem!"

Power Phrase:
"You're welcome."

**Theory:**

This might seem like an obvious one, but listen. Listen to how many times you hear "You're welcome" vs. how many times you hear "Thank you." People say *thank you* all the time. You might be surprised how little you hear people actually use the phrase "You're welcome." You'll instead hear people say things such as "No problem," "Not a problem," "You got it," "Sure," and so on. Then take note *whom* you hear actually saying, "You're welcome." You'll notice that they will consistently be confident, strong communicators.

Saying, "You're welcome" is a sign that you are accustomed to being thanked because you are accustomed to doing things for people. You are (or should be) accustomed to *giving*. It is a sign that you are *aware* that you are a giver, and happy to be so. It is a sign that you are not embarrassed to be acknowledged for your gift, whether it be of time, money, talent, attention—or anything else. People with something to offer the world, and people who truly give to others, honor the people to whom they are giving by saying "You're welcome," when they are thanked. And they say it often—habitually. It becomes a *speech pattern*--a speech pattern that distinguishes you not only as a savvy communicator, but as one who is *valuable*—and therefore makes contributions of value to the lives of others. Saying "You're welcome" is a gracious recognition that you appreciate the gratitude just expressed to you. You don't dismiss that gratitude or take it for granted. You honor *it*, and the person *extending it* to you.

*Imagine:* Oprah Winfrey surprises someone with a brand-new house. The person starts to cry and says, "Thank you, thank you Oprah." What would you imagine Oprah's response to be? Imagine her saying: "No problem! Enjoy your day!" Never. Of course not. She would say: "You're welcome." Oprah Winfrey is acknowledged as one of the greatest communicators of our day. We should all take note of the powerful communicators of our time, and implement the strategies that work for them. The principle is the same whether you give someone a house, a car, a carton of milk, the answer to a Jeopardy question, or french fries and a Coke. When you're thanked, look the grateful person right in the eye and say "You're welcome."

**Please take note--if you are in a customer service position, it's imperative that you always use "You're welcome."** This alone will separate you from the pack of novice communicators. A common mistake made by customer service professionals—one that decreases their professional power—is saying "No problem." It's sloppy, unprofessional speech, and it's *annoying* to some people. "You're welcome," is always the preferred speech pattern of savvy communicators.

### For example, notice the difference:

**SAY THIS--**"You're welcome; I'm happy I could do that for you!"
**NOT THAT--**"Not a problem!"

**SAY THIS--**"You're very welcome."
**NOT THAT--**"That's what I'm here for."

**Furthermore, you've noticed that some people can accept a compliment, and some can't?** Let's just get that out of the way right now. Most people, *when complimented*, say *anything* other than "Thank you." Most people are uncomfortable, and some even become *hostile* when complimented. Again, this reveals how often one is complimented (or not), and how confident one is (or not). If confidence is something you struggle with, remember that sometimes you need to "fake it 'til you make it," and this may be one of those instances for you. Rather than responding shyly, or god-forbid with feigned humility, respond as strong, powerful people respond when they're told something positive about themselves—just say "Thank you." If you're getting a compliment, you no doubt deserve it, so accept it graciously. In doing so, you honor the person who is complimenting you, and you honor yourself. What communication phrase could accomplish more than that?

**For example, notice the difference:**

**SAY THIS**--"Thank you."
**NOT THAT**--"Really, you think so? I'm not sure. I'm still getting used to it."

## Quick reference card
## #15

# Lesson 16

# Danger Phrase: "What were you thinking?"

Danger Phrase:

"What were you thinking?"

"How did you think that was going to make me feel?"

"What was going through your head?"

"Did you really think..."

"Did you even stop to think..."

Power Phrase:

There is no power phrase for these...these are what we call, "hostile questions."

**Theory:**

We've all done it--asked someone something such as, "How did you think that was going to make me feel? What were you thinking?" These are called, "hostile questions."

There is no good answer to a hostile question. The reason there is no good answer is because they weren't designed to be answered to begin with. They really aren't questions. They are statements--hostile, aggressive, or passive-aggressive ones--disguised as questions. When we use hostile questions, we are "setting people up" and *we* are the ones who inevitably fail.

**Furthermore, when you are about to ask a hostile question (you know because you're beginning a sentence with something like, "Why would you...?" and you're really not looking for an *answer*) STOP.** Instead, ask yourself, "What message do I really want to send here?" Once you determine what clear, direct message you want to send, send that instead. A great sign that you are asking a hostile question, therefore sabotaging your own communication success, is that you're asking it out of anger. The purpose of a question should be to gain information that leads to understanding--and nothing more.

### For example, notice the difference:

**SAY THIS**--"In the future, if you want to talk to my client, I'm asking you to run that by me first, OK?"
**NOT THAT**--"Why would you call my client without asking me first?"

**SAY THIS**--"If you are going to fix an appliance here at home, would you please let me know first, so I can help you find the right manual and tools?
**NOT THAT**--"What makes you think you can fix that

washer?"

**SAY THIS--**"When you don't tell me you're going to be late, I worry. In the future, if you just let me know you're running late, I can understand that, and there won't be any problem at all."
**NOT THAT--**"Did you even think about how I'd feel—wondering where you were?"

One last thing: Eliminating hostile questions from our communication MO can be difficult for some of us. Remember that communication skills are *learned*; they don't just come naturally. If you find yourself asking hostile questions you can always stop and apologize. We can all relate to: "What on earth was going through your head? Wait...I apologize...I shouldn't have said that. What I meant was, in the future, please come to me and discuss it before you ask your mother to come and stay with us, OK?"

There are very few people who are unsympathetic to our genuine apology when we make a communication mistake.

**For example, notice the difference:**

**SAY THIS**--"It may not have worked this time, but I still support you and am willing to help however I can."

**NOT THAT**--"Did you really think that would work?"

## Quick reference card
## #16

# Lesson 17
# THE Top 4 Power Phrases

## THE TOP 4 POWER PHRASES
## OF ALL TIME:

"That's interesting; tell me more."

"That's interesting; why would you say that?"

"That's interesting; why would you do that?"

"That's interesting; why would you ask that?"

### Theory:

We've all found ourselves at a loss for words; it happens to even the most savvy communicators. It's difficult to be in the response mode (rather than the reaction mode) *all* the time. Is it possible to always have a savvy response that covers almost every situation—and almost every time?

It is if you have a few good power phrases in your arsenal—and if you've practiced them to the point of being able to deliver them spontaneously. Think of those figure skaters that twirl and leap and jump and glide. Don't they make it look easy and fluid—as though they never have to practice, because it all comes so naturally? Yet any figure skater will stress one thing above all others—practice. Being an accomplished communicator is no different. The best ones make it look easy because they practice.

Of course we can all think of unenlightened responses to unenlightened comments and questions; this doesn't require any level of communication skill. To be able to respond to anything with tact, power, and finesse, however, is a sure sign or an educated, powerful, savvy communicator.

**Furthermore, these four power phrases can be used for many different reasons**. For example, as a savvy communicator you already know the rule that *what gets rewarded gets repeated*. Many times difficult people *keep repeating* their difficult behavior around you because they *keep getting* a reaction out of you; you are *rewarding* them with your goat.... Always remember that the savvy communicator practices goat-hiding with difficult people. No one can get your goat if they don't know where it is. So one good reason to memorize these phrases is to prevent people from getting to you—or at least prevent them from *knowing* when they do! There are many many other good reasons to use these phrases and you'll see a few as you read along.

Although these four phrases seem simple, you'll notice that they're used almost exclusively by savvy communicators.

Furthermore, they are some of the most under-used and most powerful phrases in the English language. Think about it, when was the last time someone told you what you had to say was interesting, and that they wanted to hear more of it?

Practice saying these phrases when you don't need them, and they'll come easily when you do.

### For example, notice the difference:

**SAY THIS**--"That's interesting; tell me more"
**NOT THAT**--"How could you possibly think that?" (This is a great one for people looking to argue about religion or politics. By saying "that's interesting; tell me more" you allow them to speak, without revealing your position and falling into argument-mode. The purpose of a savvy communicator in these situations, after all, is generally to gather information. What could be better than this simple phrase?)

**SAY THIS**--"That's interesting; why would you say that?"
**NOT THAT**--"Are you serious?" (Just about any time someone makes a statement that takes you off-guard, you can use this one. It is effective at work and at home as long as your intention is ***truly to learn why*** *the person is saying whatever it is he or she is saying.*)

**SAY THIS**--"That's interesting; why would you ask me that?"

**NOT THAT**--"It's none of your business." (This stops the challenger every time. BTW, if the challenger persists by saying: "I'm just curious,"--use *the broken record* —"That's interesting; are you always this curious? Tell me more."

**SAY THIS**--"That's interesting; why would you do that?"

**NOT THAT**--"What's wrong with you?" (This is a good one for managers and supervisors being challenged by employees, or when we are suspicious of destructive behavior. Remember: ask first **with the purpose of understanding**.)

Though each phrase is accompanied by one situation for its use, there are in fact thousands of situations in which these phrases will be effective for you. Think about it, and remember to practice these power phrases until you are able to deliver them effortlessly even in an emotionally charged moment—when the logical side of your brain is giving way to the emotional side. That's why you memorize these phrases—so that you don't have to think about a "clever response" to shut down the person bothering you. These phrases will magically appear, if you are prepared to use them.

**For example, notice the difference:**

**SAY THIS**--"That's interesting; why would you do that?"
**NOT THAT**--"Did you really think that would work?" (So many uses for this one—at work and at home.)

## Quick reference card
## #17

# Lesson 18

# Danger Phrase: "We need to talk."

Danger Phrase:

"We need to talk"

Power Phrase:

"(*Person's name*), I need your help."

**Theory:**

If your intention is to close down the lines of communication, the phrase, "We need to talk," is one of the best ways to do it.

People--especially men--have connected so much negativity to this phrase that most of us literally have a physical reaction when we hear it. This phrase causes a strong bio-chemical reaction in the listener, and the lines of communication promptly shut down. Again, this has to do mostly with the association we've made with this phrase. I mean, no one in the history of the universe has ever said, "Honey, we need to talk. I just bought you a **brand new car**!" Never. It doesn't happen. We all know what "We need to talk" leads to, and it's not pretty.

When we need to have one of "those little talks" with someone, the first goal we should have is to open the lines of communication so the person is *ready to receive* the message that we intend to convey. The easiest way to do that is to use this simple 3-step process:

**Step 1: Use the person's name.**
**Step 2: Make the sentence short.**
**Step 3: Use "I" language. (Say something about *you* first--not the other person's behavior.)**

These three steps can be easily summarized and implemented using two different lead-in lines ("starter" phrases that help you get the words out):
Lead-in Line #1: "_____, I need your help."
Lead-in Line #2: "_____, I'm concerned," or "_____, I'm frustrated," or "_____, I'm troubled."

**Furthermore, having a plan, and "scripting" out the first sentence of "those little talks" will help boost** your confidence and effectiveness. If you start out weakly, the listener pays no attention to you; if you start off too aggressively, the lines of communication shut down. Using the 3-step process or one of the lead-in lines above will help ensure that you come off neither aggressive nor passive--but rather *perfectly assertive*.

## For example, notice the difference:

**SAY THIS**--"John, I need your help."
**NOT THAT**--"John, we need to talk."

**SAY THIS**--"John, I'm concerned and could really use your help."
**NOT THAT**--"John, you need to start carrying your weight around here."

**SAY THIS**--"John, I'm troubled and I need your help."
**NOT THAT**--"Listen John, we need to talk; you really messed up."

Remember that the purpose of the lead-in to "*the talk*" is to open the lines of communication and get the person's *buy-in* to your message. Our ego sometimes wants the other person to squirm at the beginning of the conversation. While this might temporarily feed our ego, it's not the effective thing to do. If the other person is engaging in self-talk because of his concern about what's coming—he will be listening to himself—not to you.

**For example, notice the difference:**

**SAY THIS**--"John, I'm concerned; we need to tackle a few problems."
**NOT THAT**--"John, close the door and sit down."

## Quick reference card
## #18

# Lesson 19
# Power Phrase: "You're in Luck!"

Power Phrase:

"You're in luck!"

## Theory:

Want to produce a positive bio-chemical reaction in someone else's body?

As we've discussed in previous lessons, everything people say to us has a physical effect on us, and everything we say to other people has a physical effect on them (something to remember—especially when we speak to children.) Sometimes the effect is minimal, such as when we hear, "What would you like to drink?" and sometimes it's substantial. For example, imagine hearing: "I'm going to kill you." Any way you want to cut it, words have power and they do evoke a response in the hearer.

Many times we are dealing with people who are frustrated, angry, or in some way difficult, and we need a quick way to "win them over." One simple way to do that is to tell them that they're lucky! Notice how advertisers will use phrases such as, "You're in luck America! We've extended our promotion for one more week!" or "You're in luck if you're aged 65-99, because you are eligible for our 'young at heart' discount." Advertisers do this so that you will associate the good feeling you get while reading or hearing the phrase, "You're in luck!"--with their product.

For example, let's imagine that you have to deliver bad news to a customer. Perhaps their package will be a day late. Let's assume you know that it's really not a big deal to them, but it's not what they were hoping for, either. Instead of simply saying something such as, "I'm really sorry, but your package won't be arriving until tomorrow," try something savvy such as, "Dan, I just found out that our package won't be arriving until tomorrow. But having said that— you're in luck because on late orders—even just one day late--I can refund you the entire shipping amount. How does that sound?"

Of course, we have to use caution when using this advanced tactic. You can tell if a customer is just a little annoyed, or really angry. This tactic is great if you think someone is on-the-fence about getting angry. It's also wonderful if the compensation you're offering will obviously outweigh the inconvenience. ***It's not a great one to use when all has gone wrong.*** For example, I wouldn't recommend a veterinarian say: "You're in luck! Your dog's dead, so that means you won't have to buy any more dog food!" If you're savvy enough to be reading this, you're savvy enough to discern when it is--and is not—appropriate to begin with "You're in luck."

**Furthermore, for customer service representatives, here's a general rule for the "You're in luck" phrase.** Are you in a position to assist this person? If so—ipso facto—the person is in luck. So tell him/her so. However, if you have nothing to deliver but bad news, and you cannot help—the person is not in luck, so eliminate the phrase. Having said that—don't forget that as a de-fuser of the angry person who is frustrated because he thinks no one can help him—yet you know that you can—start with "You're in luck" and then prove it by providing excellent customer service! And if you want to ice the cake, add "You've found the right person." Then, *be* the right person to help.

### For example, notice the difference:

**SAY THIS**--"Mr. Jones, you're in luck! Because it will be a few more minutes until your room is ready, you can go ahead and enjoy free beverages in our lounge while we get the room made up for you."
**NOT THAT**--"It'll be just a few minutes until your room is ready. I can offer you some free drinks in the lounge while you wait."

**SAY THIS**--"That sounds totally frustrating, but Mr. Jones--you're in luck. You've found the right person; I'm Dan O'Connor, and I can help you with this."
**NOT THAT**--"Who told you that?"

**SAY THIS**--"Well, that weekend is unfortunately sold out, but you're in luck. I have an even better room the following weekend that I can give you at the same price if you'd like."
**NOT THAT**--"No, I'm sorry, we're totally sold out." (Remember, always try to find a positive that will balance the negative news.)

While we're on the topic of customer service, remember that "Do you want...?" is also a delete phrase, and we should instead use, "Would you like...?"

**For example, notice the difference:**

**SAY THIS**--"Would you like a bag with that?"
**NOT THAT**--"Do you want a bag?"

## Quick reference card
## #19

# Lesson 20
# Danger Phrase: "You said..."

Danger Phrase:
"You Said..."

Power Phrase:
"I heard..." or "I understood..."

### Theory:

As we learned in lesson 14, over 50% of the time people say something other than *what they think they're saying*. With that in mind, the savvy communicator knows that what people do (or don't) say is nearly irrelevant when it comes to understanding the truth. Furthermore, it's a waste of time to try and prove that someone either did or did not say something, because our goal shouldn't be to prove or disprove the past; the goal should be to seek understanding in and about the present.

So why do we constantly hear people start sentences with, "You said," or "But you told me," and other variations of that phrase? Because most people are not savvy communicators.

With that said, of course some of us love a good fight. If what you're looking for is a good argument, then go ahead and say, "Wait! You just said..." which is aggressive and hostile.

**Furthermore, this phrase increases self-talk.**
Whether someone expresses it or not, when we say to people, "But yesterday you told me..." their self-talk starts to race through yesterday and reconstruct the past. They become defensive, and frequently mold their memory of what they said to fit what they *think they should have said*, and the fresh mold becomes the new memory. The worst part? They do all of this while they should be listening to us, but can't, because they're too busy with all the self-talk caused by our "You told me..." phrase. For selfish reasons, it's best if we just leave what *they said* out of it. This increases the odds of actual *listening* taking place.

Remember--when most people say, "I did NOT say that!" they *believe* they didn't, even if in fact they did. How are we supposed to argue against that? And why would we want to? If you believe someone said one thing and did another, or if you *know* that someone in fact lied to you, what good does it to to "prove" it? Better to know who you're dealing with and plan your communication accordingly. Period.

The goal, as we mentioned before, should be *understanding*, right? If you want people to *understand* you, and you want to *understand* others, talk about what *you heard or understood* instead of what *they said*. **Talking about what you *heard* slows down self-talk** so your message has a better chance of getting through. Remember that the moment we say, "You said..." or any version of it, the other person's self-talk will start racing as they think, "I did NOT say that! Did I? What did I say?" That is *not* conducive to active listening.

**For example, notice the difference:**

**SAY THIS**--"That's interesting; let me clarify what I heard before I respond, OK?"
**NOT THAT**--"So you're saying you're better than me?"

**SAY THIS**--"I'm confused. Yesterday I understood that before you left you were going to clean the basement."
**NOT THAT**--"Hey, you promised you were going to clean that basement."

**SAY THIS**--"So what I'm hearing is that you are uncomfortable working with John. Is that correct?"
**NOT THAT**--"So you're saying you hate John?"

**SAY THIS**--"I thought that after the play, we were going to go to dinner."

**NOT THIS**--"You promised to take me to dinner after the play."

Start noticing how the savvy, powerful communicators you know talk about what *they heard* rather than what *others say;* then you do the same. You'll notice an immediate difference in your communication results.

**For example, notice the difference:**

**SAY THIS**--"Oh, I heard something different."

**NOT THAT**--"You are a liar."

## Quick reference card
## #20

# Lesson 21
# The Most Crucial Phrases of All Time
## I saved the most important Danger and Power Phrases for last.

All of us either have children, will have children, or were children. All of us have occasion to be around children. The following phrases were written for parents and guardians, but to some extent they pertain to every one of us who interacts with children—and that would be all of us. And don't we want all children to grow up to be happy, healthy, productive, and well-adjusted? To that end, I've outlined 5 Danger Phrases and 10 Power Phrases, just for the children in our lives.

## Danger Phrases:

1. "Not good enough."

2. "Why can't you be more like..."

3. "I am so fat—or stupid—or incompetent"

4. "I'm ashamed of you."

5. "You're a ___er."

# Power Phrases:

1. "I love you so much—no matter what—always."
2. "You can always count on me."
3. "You're beautiful just the way you are."
4. "Your job is to dream as big as you can. My job is to help you achieve your dreams. I'll do my job if you do yours."
5. "You can do it. You can do anything."
6. "Failure is just one step closer to the solution. Everybody fails.
The only real failure is not trying. Failure is just part of the process—
it means you're doing it right."
7. "Being courageous doesn't mean not being afraid, it means doing what's right even though you're afraid."
8. "You're never alone. I'll always be here for you."
9. "Why not?"
10. "You're perfect."

Now, let's break it down:

# 5 Danger Phrases Your Children Should NEVER Hear You Say

1) **"Not good enough."** Children look to their parents for validation of who they are and how much they're worth. For children it's parents first, **then** God. Give your children the gift of self-esteem. Children find it difficult to separate *what they do* from *who they are*. We might think we're telling our children that they didn't try hard enough, or that their homework wasn't good enough, but what they hear is that **they aren't enough**. As a parent, you have the power to change your child's world forever with just one word. **Enough** can be that word. When you're about to criticize your child's work, try wrapping it in a compliment, such as, "You're good enough to win the gold medal the next time if you keep practicing," or "you're smart enough to get an A the next time if you just keep studying." Imagine if tomorrow God came down from heaven and told you that you are good enough, strong enough, smart enough, and pretty enough just the way you are. You can make that happen for your kids starting right now. What a gift, huh?

2) **"Why can't you be more like (your brother, your sister, John, Mike, Trixie?)..."** is a total spirit-killer. Don't speak words of death. We all know what it's like and how it hurts to be compared to other people. Your children will do enough of that in their own heads when they grow

up. We all do. When you feel like comparing your children to other people, instead, choose the characteristics that you admire in the people you were about to use as comparisons, and compliment your kids on those characteristics. For example, "You know John, when I see you applying yourself to your school work, it really makes me proud of you." Or, "When I see the loving side of you come out when you're with your little sister, I feel so proud to be your mother that my heart nearly bursts."

3) **"I am so fat–or stupid–or incompetent"** or any version of that, including, "It's hell getting old; I need a face-lift," or any other self-degrading comments. If you have self-esteem issues, the surest way to pass those issues to your children is to talk about them in front of your children. Remember, our children model our behavior. That's a fact and the truth. The words you use to describe yourself become part of their internal programming. Remember, you are everything to your child. When you say, "I am," It's going to turn out to mean, "We are," and ultimately, "I am" in your child's mind. Any phrase you use to describe yourself will be planted in their brain, and will be the phrase they use. If you say something along the lines of, "I'm fat and ugly," It's like a magic spell you cast, and when your child reaches your age, he or she will look in the mirror and say the exact same thing. Watch what you say about yourself in front of your kids. If you want to give your children the gift of self-esteem, say positive things

about yourself as well as positive things about them. Look in the mirror in front of your child and let them hear you say beautiful things about yourself. If this is difficult for you, start by saying things to your child such as, "You know, when I look at you, it makes me feel beautiful, because you're beautiful, and you're part of me." And eventually you'll reach the point where you can compliment yourself, as well as others.

**4) "I'm ashamed of you."** This is a delete phrase. There is never a good reason to hurt our children, and that's the only thing this phrase accomplishes. It would be better to kick your child in the face…it would do less damage. If you feel like using this phrase, instead, try something along the lines of: "When you ___ it hurts me." You can elaborate if you have a dramatic streak, and say things along the lines of, "When you ___ it's like a knife being plunged through my heart, and I feel as though I'm dying a slow, painful death," But the basic pattern is, "When you ___ I feel ___."

**5) "You're a ___er."** (Fill in the blank with any word that isn't positive.) We can change a child forever with just one word. Children are made of words. We tell our children what they are. Every single word spoken to a child becomes a part of who they are, and once a word is spoken, there is no taking it back. If you're going to label your children, make sure your labels are kind and loving. Any time you start a phrase with, "You're a…" from this point forward you have two choices: put in a positive word, such as, "lover, creative thinker, helper, do-gooder" or stop speaking before you kill with your words. Any negative word that ends in – er, or any other negative label is toxic for children, and kills them a little. Don't kill your own children or anyone else's either.

# 10 POWER PHRASES YOUR CHILDREN SHOULD HEAR YOU SAY OFTEN.

**Use these phrases constantly. You can't say them enough. Say them to your kids--right now as soon as you finish reading this--and never stop saying them.**

Communication skills are not just about business. The most important place you can exhibit effective communication skills is at home. Here are some power phrases you can use at home, or in the homes of friends, in abundance. Use them all the time, every day.

**1. "I love you so much–no matter what–always."**
And I won't love you more or less when your report card comes out, when you choose a boyfriend, when you pass that test.

**2. "You can always count on me."** Even when you're in trouble—even when you've disappointed me—even when you've made so many mistakes the neighbors will never stop talking.

**3. "You're beautiful just the way you are."** And I'll feel that way about you with or without the nose job, the extra fat around your middle, the cowlick you can't comb....

**4. "Your job is to dream as big as you can. My job is to help you achieve your dreams. I'll do my job if you do yours."** And I'll recognize that your dreams for you may be different from my dreams for you. Yours are what matter.

**5. "You can do it. You can do anything."** The only limits you have are those you place on yourself.

**6. "Failure is just one step closer to the solution. Everybody fails. The only real failure is not trying. Failure is just part of the process—it means you're doing it right."** I'll help lift the boulder of disillusionment from your shoulders whenever failure makes you want to quit. I'll remind you of all the inventors who saw their failures as moving them one step closer to the solution.

**7. "Being courageous doesn't mean not being afraid, it means doing what's right even though**

**you're afraid."** Ask any soldier who's been in battle; he or she was afraid. Ask any person who has been in the public arena, trying to perform in front of the crowd; he or she was afraid. Ask any brave person who committed heroic deeds; you'll find that he or she was afraid. Fear comes hand in hand with courage. It's when you overcome your fear and ACT—that you are courageous. Opportunities present themselves quietly and consistently every single day. Courageous people are all around us, making life better. I'll help you be one of those people.

**8. "You're never alone. I'll always be here for you."** You are mine; I am yours. Nothing, not even death, can ever change that. Nothing you do will ever change that. Our bond is forever; it's a miracle of the love we share.

**9. "Why not?"** You don't deserve it? Why not? You can't do it? Why not? I'll always help you see the possibilities that are before you.

**10. "You're perfect."** You'd better believe it. Just as you are—you are perfect in my eyes, as surely as though I were the God who created you. Now go out and manifest that perfection and change the world.

# Quick reference card
## #What's Next?

It was my intention, throughout these 21 lessons, to furnish you with many new tools for your communication arsenal, and give you a new perspective on communication training itself. Communication training is a life-long process; you should never stop looking, listening, learning, and incorporating the best approaches, tips, techniques, scripts, and strategies into your everyday interaction with people. The fact that you read this book tells me it is your goal to be a savvy communicator; I wrote this book because it is my goal to help become one.

You'll find the daily reminder cards in the Customer Resources section of our website. Simply go to www.danoconnortraining.com, and in the Communication Training drop-down menu, you'll see the Customer Resources link. Click there, you'll find the quick-reference cards that accompany these lessons. You can use one of these cards a day, one a week, or one when the spirit moves you. Once you make the techniques listed on these 21 cards your own—through practice, practice, practice, you will be well on your way to confident, savvy communication.

Please be sure to visit our communication training website at http://www.danoconnortraining.com for more communication training tools such as books, blogs, audios, and videos--and follow us on Facebook (/communicationtraining) and Twitter (EVSlayer).

If you need any help, or are looking to bring a motivational keynote speaker or expert communication trainer to your next event, you can contact me directly at dan@danoconnortraining.com, or 877-570-1573 in the US, or 701-205-4141 outside the US.

I'm honored that you would let me into your world, and look forward to a long, fruitful relationship.

Dan O'Connor

Chim-Kow-Kwoo

## ABOUT THE AUTHOR

Communication expert Dan O'Connor has been helping individuals and organizations develop their communication and critical thinking skills for over fifteen years. Recognized both nationally and internationally, Dan came to prominence through his development and delivery of programs that include dealing with difficult and demanding people, understanding and dealing with different personality types, speaking with power and precision, professional communication and etiquette, developing your personal compass, transformational thinking, customer service scripts and techniques, team-building and many many more—all programs based on self-development and powerful communication.

Having witnessed the business problems caused by office energy vampires, workplace negativity, interpersonal conflicts, and employees and supervisors struggling to "find the words," Dan began developing tactical training programs that go beyond theory, and focus on scripts, phrases, communication systems, and memory techniques designed to deliver instant results.

The instant results? Transformation--both personal and professional.

Dan has produced countless personal and professional communication training resources, including top-rated blogs, seminars, articles, and more. His latest works include Energy Vampire Slaying:101 (dealing with difficult people program), his online training course www.onlinecommunicationtraining.com, and his youtube channel www.youtube.com/PowerDiversity.

Dan travels out of Fargo, ND, USA, and can be reached at dan@danoconnortraining.com.

*Look for our next Say This--NOT THAT book,*

*Say This--NOT THAT **to your spouse***

# Quick reference card #1

## Danger Phrase:
## "I'm sorry."
## Power Phrase:
## "I apologize."

**SAY THIS--** "I apologize for arriving so late."

**NOT THAT--**"I'm sorry that I arrived so late."

**SAY THIS--**"I apologize for forgetting your birthday."

**NOT THAT--**"I'm sorry I forgot your birthday."

**SAY THIS--**"I apologize for being rude to you in front of your friends."

**NOT THAT--**"I'm sorry I was rude to you in front of your friends."

**SAY THIS--**"I apologize **for** hurting your feelings; please forgive me."

**NOT THAT--**"I apologize **if** I hurt your feelings."

*These cards can also be printed from the customer resources section of our website, www.danoconnortraining.com.*

# Quick reference card #2

**Danger Phrase:**
**"Calm down."**

**Power Phrase:**
**"I understand..."**

**SAY THIS**--"I understand how upset you are, and I can help."

**NOT THAT**--"I can't help you until you calm down!"

**SAY THIS**--"I understand why you would feel that way; please give me a chance to help.

**NOT THAT**--"Please calm down and I'll be able to help you."

**SAY THIS**--"I can certainly understand why you'd be so upset."

**NOT THAT**--"I understand exactly how you feel."

*These cards can also be printed from the customer resources section of our website, www.danoconnortraining.com.*

# Quick reference card #3

**Danger Phrase:**
**"I have an idea."**

**Power Phrase:**
**"I have an answer."**

**SAY THIS**--"I have the answer to this problem."

**NOT THAT**--"I have an idea about how we can fix this problem."

**SAY THIS**--"I have an answer I believe will work."

**NOT THAT**--"I have an idea I think will work."

**SAY THIS**--"I've come up with a few proposals for you."

**NOT THAT**--"I've come up with a few ideas for you."

**SAY THIS**--"I believe I have the solution."

**NOT THAT**--"I think I have an idea."

*These cards can also be printed from the customer resources section of our website, www.danoconnortraining.com.*

# Quick reference card #4

**Danger Phrase:**
**"What's wrong with you?"**

**Power Phrase:**
**"What's bothering you?"**

**SAY THIS--**"What's bothering you so much that you would say something like that?"
**NOT THAT--**"Why would you say that? What's wrong with you?"
**SAY THIS--**"What's upsetting you?"
**NOT THAT--**"What's your problem?"
**SAY THIS--**"I'm here for you, if you ever want to talk about it."
**NOT THAT--**"Do you want to talk about it?" *(Assume a "No.")* "Are you sure??"

*These cards can also be printed from the customer resources section of our website, www.danoconnortraining.com.*

97

# Quick reference card
# #5

**Danger Phrase:**
**"My name is..."**
**Power Phrase:**
**"I'm..."**

**SAY THIS--** "Hi, I'm Dan O'Connor."
**NOT THAT--**"Hi, my name's Dan
O'Connor."
**SAY THIS--**"It's nice to meet you Mary; I'm
Dan."
**NOT THAT--**"It's nice to meet you, Mary; my
name's Dan."
**SAY THIS--** "Hi, this is Dan O'Connor, with
Power Diversity; is Mary in?"
**NOT THIS--**"Hi, My name's Dan O'Connor,
with Power Diversity; is Mary in?"
**SAY THIS--**"Hi Mark, this is Jim Schmith,
Commercial Realtor with Goldmark."
**NOT THIS--**"Hi Mark, my name is Jim
Schmith. I'm a Commercial Realtor with
Goldmark."

*These cards can also be printed from the*
*customer resources section of our website,*
*www.danoconnortraining.com.*

# Quick reference card #6

### Danger Phrase:
### "I disagree."
### Power Phrase:
### "I see it another way."

**SAY THIS--**"I understand what you're saying; I simply see it another way."

**NOT THAT--**"I understand what you're saying; I just disagree."

**SAY THIS--**"I understand how you see it; I simply see it differently.

**NOT THAT--**"You make a good point, but I disagree with you."

**SAY THIS--**"I see it differently, however this is interesting; tell me more if you like."

**NOT THAT--**"I totally disagree."

**SAY THIS--**"I can understand how you see it; I see it another way; however I trust your judgment and you have my support."

**NOT THAT--**"Let's just agree to disagree."

*These cards can also be printed from the customer resources section of our website, www.danoconnortraining.com.*

# Quick reference card #7

**Danger Phrase:**
**"Our Computers are slow."**
**Power Phrase:**
**"While we're waiting for the computer to process...."**

**SAY THIS--**"While we're waiting for the computer to process, tell me, how has your experience been with us so far?"

**NOT THAT--**"I'm sorry; our computers are really slow today."

**SAY THIS--**"While the information is coming up, could you please tell me why you chose to work with us?"

**NOT THAT--**"Please give me a minute while the computer comes up."

**SAY THIS--**"Unfortunately our computers are down, but fortunately you got me, Dan O'Connor, and I'm going to help you as best I can. Tell me about...."

**NOT THAT--**"Unfortunately our computers are down right now."

*These cards can also be printed from the customer resources section of our website, www.danoconnortraining.com.*

# Quick reference card #8

## Danger Phrase:
## "Why didn't you tell me?"
## Power Phrase:
## "In the future, you can always come to me with these things."

**SAY THIS--**"You know, in the future, you can always come to me with these things."

**NOT THAT--**"Why didn't you tell me what was going on?"

**SAY THIS--**"In the future, I hope you know you can always come to me with these things and I won't get defensive, or put you on the offensive, either."

**NOT THAT--**"Why didn't you tell me how that made you feel?"

**SAY THIS--**"In the future, you can always come to me with these things and know that I won't judge you when you do."

**NOT THAT--**"Why didn't you tell me what you were doing?"

*These cards can also be printed from the customer resources section of our website, www.danoconnortraining.com.*

# Quick reference card #9

## Danger Phrase:
## "But..."
## Power Phrase:
## "Having said that..."

**SAY THIS**--"I trust you. Having said that, I can't do what you're asking."

**NOT THAT**--"I trust you, **but** I can't do what you're asking."

**SAY THIS**--"I've always enjoyed working with you. That said, I have to move on."

**NOT THAT**--"I've always enjoyed working with you, **but** I have to move on."

**SAY THIS**--"I understand what you're saying. Having said that, I see it another way."

**NOT THAT**--"I understand what you're saying, **but** I simply disagree."

**SAY THIS**--"While I love you, I can't do that for you."

**NOT THAT**--"I love you, **but** I can't do that for you."

*These cards can also be printed from the customer resources section of our website, www.danoconnortraining.com.*

# Quick reference card #10

**Danger Phrase:**
**"No offense but…"**
**"Don't take this the wrong way but…"**
**"I don't mean to be rude but…"**

**Power Phrase:**
There is no power phrase you can use to replace these; they are simply DELETE phrases.

**SAY THIS--**"You're too polished a professional to let something like a personality conflict tarnish your image."
**NOT THAT--**"Don't take this the wrong way, but you need to stop fighting with Trixie."
**SAY THIS--**"You've worked too hard on this report to let errors distract from the message."
**NOT THAT--**"I don't mean to be rude, but this report is full of errors."

*These cards can also be printed from the customer resources section of our website, www.danoconnortraining.com.*

# Quick reference card #11

**Danger Phrase:**

**"Our policy..."**

**Power Phrase:**

**"The reason our policy states _____ is because..."**

**SAY THIS--** "I understand this can be frustrating, but we have these procedures in place to protect your account from fraud. That's why we ask you to deliver your application in person—for your protection."

**NOT THAT--** "I'm sorry, but our company policy states you must deliver your application in person rather than by fax or mail—no exceptions."

**SAY THIS--** "Unfortunately, we have to have uniform policies like this so we can keep your rates as low as possible."

**NOT THAT--** "Company policy states that if you don't pay your bill by the 7th, your service will be cut off."

*These cards can also be printed from the customer resources section of our website, www.danoconnortraining.com.*

# Quick reference card #12

## Danger Phrase:
## "I need..."

## Power Phrase:
### *Place the real subject at the beginning of the sentence.*

**SAY THIS--** "That report is due by the end of the day."

**NOT THAT--**"I need that report by the end of the day."

**SAY THIS--** "This class deserves your full attention."

**NOT THAT--**"I want you to pay attention in class."

**SAY THIS--**"Your complete focus is vital to the success of this project."

**NOT THAT--**"I need you to really focus on this project."

*These cards can also be printed from the customer resources section of our website, www.danoconnortraining.com.*

# Quick reference card #13

### Danger Phrase:
### "Honestly..." or "To be honest"

### Power Phrase:
### "Frankly..."

**SAY THIS--** "Frankly, it's difficult for me to see how this is going to work."

**NOT THAT--**"Honestly, it's difficult for me to see how this is going to work."

**SAY THIS--**"Would you like me to be frank?"

**NOT THAT--**"Would you like me to be honest?"

**SAY THIS--** "I liked the way the report was laid out. Next time I'd use primary colors rather than fluorescent colors because they're easier on the eyes."

**NOT THAT--** "I hated the fluorescent colors. I'd get rid of them and use primary colors instead. I'm just being honest here."

*These cards can also be printed from the customer resources section of our website, www.danoconnortraining.com.*

# Quick reference card #14

### Danger Phrase:
### "You make me..."

### Power Phrase:
### "When you...I feel...because..."

**SAY THIS--** "When you don't do what you say you'll do, I feel disappointed and hurt because I love you and try to do what I tell you I'll do."

**NOT THAT--** "You know, you really make me mad when you don't do what you say you're going to do."

**SAY THIS--** "When you talk to me like that-- calling me names--in front of our friends, I feel embarrassed and humiliated because it reminds me of when I was name-called on the playground as a child."

**NOT THAT--** "That really pisses me off when you do that."

*These cards can also be printed from the customer resources section of our website, www.danoconnortraining.com.*

# Quick reference card #15

**Danger Phrase:**
**"No problem..."**

**Power Phrase:**
**"You're welcome."**

**SAY THIS--** "You're welcome; I'm happy I could do that for you!"
**NOT THAT--**"Not a problem!"
**SAY THIS--** "You're very welcome."
**NOT THAT--**"That's what I'm here for."
**SAY THIS--** "Thank you."
**NOT THAT--** "Really, you think so? I'm not sure. I'm still getting used to it."

*These cards can also be printed from the customer resources section of our website, www.danoconnortraining.com.*

# Quick reference card #16

**Danger Phrase:**
**"What were you thinking?"**
**"How did you think that was going to make me feel?"**
**"What was going through your head?"**
**"Did you really think..."**
**"Did you even stop to think..."**
**Power Phrase:**
**There is no power phrase for these...these are what we call, "hostile questions."**

**SAY THIS--**"In the future, if you want to talk to my client, I'm asking you to run that by me first, OK?"
**NOT THAT--**"Why would you call my client without asking me first?"

*These cards can also be printed from the customer resources section of our website, www.danoconnortraining.com.*

# Quick reference card #17

## 4 MAGIC POWER PHRASES

*"That's interesting; tell me more."*
**"That's interesting; why would you say that?"**
**"That's interesting; why would you do that?"**
**"That's interesting; why would you ask that?"**

**SAY THIS--** "That's interesting; tell me more"
**NOT THAT--**"How could you possibly think that?"
**SAY THIS--**"That's interesting; why would you say that?"
**NOT THAT--**"Are you serious?"
**SAY THIS--**"That's interesting; why would you ask me that?"
**NOT THAT--**"It's none of your business."
**SAY THIS--**"That's interesting; why would you do that?"
**NOT THAT--**"What's wrong with you?"

*These cards can also be printed from the customer resources section of our website, www.danoconnortraining.com.*

110

# Quick reference card #18

**Danger Phrase:**
**"We need to talk"**
**Power Phrase:**
**"(*Person's name*), I need your help."**

**SAY THIS--** "John, I need your help."
**NOT THAT--**"John, we need to talk."
**SAY THIS--**"John, I'm concerned and could really use your help."
**NOT THAT--** "John, you need to start carrying your weight around here."
**SAY THIS--**"John, I'm troubled and I need your help."
**NOT THAT--**"Listen John, we need to talk; you really messed up."
**SAY THIS--**"John, I'm concerned; we need to tackle a few problems."
**NOT THAT--**"John, close the door and sit down."

*These cards can also be printed from the customer resources section of our website, www.danoconnortraining.com.*

# Quick reference card #19

## Power Phrase:
## "You're in luck!"

**SAY THIS--** "Mr. Jones, you're in luck! Because it will be a few more minutes until your room is ready, you can go ahead and enjoy free beverages in our lounge while we get it made up for you."

**NOT THAT--** "It'll be just a few minutes until your room is ready. I can offer you some free drinks in the lounge while you wait."

**SAY THIS--** "That sounds totally frustrating, but Mr. Jones--you're in luck. You've found the right person; I'm Dan O'Connor, and I can help you with this."

**NOT THAT--** "Who told you that?"

**SAY THIS--** "Well, that weekend is unfortunately sold out, but you're in luck. I have an even better room the following weekend that I can give you at the same price if you'd like."

**NOT THAT--** "No, I'm sorry, we're totally sold out."

*These cards can also be printed from the customer resources section of our website, www.danoconnortraining.com.*

# Quick reference card #20

### Danger Phrase:
### "You Said..."

### Power Phrase:
### "I heard" or "I understood..."

**SAY THIS--** "That's interesting; let me clarify what I heard before I respond, OK?"

**NOT THAT--**"Did you just say you're better than me?"

**SAY THIS--**"I'm confused. Yesterday I understood that before you left you were going to clean the basement."

**NOT THAT--**"Hey, you promised you were going to clean that basement."

**SAY THIS--**"So what I'm hearing is that you are uncomfortable working with John. Is that correct?"

**NOT THAT--** "So you're saying you hate John?"

*These cards can also be printed from the customer resources section of our website, www.danoconnortraining.com.*

# Quick reference card #21

## Danger Phrases:
## (TO BE AVOIDED UNTIL THE END OF TIME)

1. "Not good enough"
2. "Why can't you be more like..."
3. "I am so fat–or stupid–or incompetent."
4. "I'm ashamed of you."
5. "You're a ___er."

*These cards can also be printed from the customer resources section of our website, www.danoconnortraining.com.*

# Quick reference card #21
## Power Phrases:

1. "I love you so much—no matter what—always."
2. "You can always count on me."
3. "You're beautiful just the way you are."
4. "Your job is to dream as big as you can. My job is to help you achieve your dreams. I'll do my job if you do yours."
5. "You can do it. You can do anything."
6. "Failure is just one step closer to the solution. Everybody fails.
The only real failure is not trying.
Failure is just part of the process—
it means you're doing it right."
7. "Being courageous doesn't mean not being afraid, it means doing what's right even though you're afraid."
8. "You're never alone. I'll always be here for you."
9. "Why not?"
10. "You're perfect."

*These cards can also be printed from the customer resources section of our website, www.danoconnortraining.com.*

*Dealing with difficult people?*

*Look for Energy Vampire Slaying: 101*
*By Dan O'Connor*

*For*
*consulting,*
*training,*
*speaking,*
*interviews,*
*and more, go to* www.danoconnortraining.com*.*

Made in the USA
Coppell, TX
02 February 2023

12015263R00066